the Blessings of OBEDIENCE

Other Titles by Andrew Murray

Abide in Christ
Absolute Surrender
Andrew Murray on Prayer
Andrew Murray on the Holy Spirit
The Blood of the Cross
Covenants and Blessings
Daily Experience with God
The Deeper Christian Life
Divine Healing
An Exciting New Life
Experiencing the Holy Spirit
Full Life in Christ
God's Best Secrets
God's Plans for You
God's Power for Today
God's Will: Our Dwelling Place
The Holiest of All
How to Strengthen Your Faith
Humility
The Joy of Being Forgiven
A Life of Power
The Master's Indwelling
The Ministry of Intercession
The Power of the Blood of Jesus
The Practice of God's Presence
Prayer Guide
Prayer Power
Raising Your Children for Christ
Reaching Your World for Christ
Receiving Power from God
The Secret of God's Presence
The Secret of Intercession
The Secret of Spiritual Strength
Secrets of Authority
The Spiritual Life
The True Vine
Waiting on God
With Christ in the School of Prayer
With Wings as Eagles

the
Blessings of
OBEDIENCE

Andrew Murray

WHITAKER
HOUSE

Publisher's note:
This new edition from Whitaker House has been edited for the modern reader. Words, expressions, and sentence structure have been updated for clarity and readability.

All Scripture quotations are taken from the King James Version of the Holy Bible.

THE BLESSINGS OF OBEDIENCE

ISBN 0-88368-842-5
Printed in the United States of America
© 1984 by Whitaker House

Whitaker House
30 Hunt Valley Circle
New Kensington, PA 15068
www.whitakerhouse.com

Library of Congress Cataloging-in-Publication Data

Murray, Andrew, 1828–1917.
The blessings of obedience / by Andrew Murray.
p.   cm.
ISBN 0-88368-842-5
1. Obedience—Religious aspects—Christianity.   2. Obedience—
Biblical teaching.   I. Title.
BV4647.O2 M873 2002
234'.6—dc21
2002012156

---

2 3 4 5 6 7 8 9 10 11 12 **UJ** 11 10 09 08 07 06 05 04

Table of Contents

Preface

This book is presented with the fervent prayer that it will please our gracious Father to use it for the instruction and strengthening of the young men and women on whom the church and the world depend. May the God of all grace bless them abundantly!

It often happens after a conference, or even after writing a book, that it is as if one only then begins to realize the meaning and importance of the truth with which one has been occupied. I feel as if I had utterly failed in grasping or expounding the spiritual character, indispensable necessity, divine and actual possibility, and the inconceivable blessings of entire obedience to our Father in heaven. Let me, therefore, summarize the main points that strike me with special power and ask every reader to note them as some of the chief lessons to be learned while growing in Christ's obedience.

Our Father in heaven expects every child of His to yield wholehearted obedience to Him. To

The Blessings of Obedience

enable His children to do this, He has made an abundant and sufficient provision in the promise of the new covenant and in the gift of His Son and Spirit. The Christian soul can enjoy God's provision and see promises fulfilled as His presence works daily in the believer.

The very entrance into this life demands the vow of absolute obedience. The new Christian agrees to surrender his whole being to be, think, speak, and do nothing but what is according to the will of God. Since these things are true, it is not enough that we agree with them. We need the Holy Spirit to give us such a vision of their glory and divine power that we will not rest until we accept everything God is willing to do for us.

Pray that God will, by the light of His Spirit, show us His loving and almighty will concerning us. Let us pray that it will be impossible for us to be disobedient to the heavenly vision.

ANDREW MURRAY

Chapter One

Obedience:
Its Place in Scripture

When studying the Bible or any Christian truth, it is always helpful to note how and when your topic occurs throughout Scripture. As you learn its place in God's pattern of Scripture, you will understand its significance in God's entire message. To prepare you to study obedience, let's look at various passages that reveal the mind of God concerning it.

"And the LORD God commanded the man," (Genesis 2:16). And later He said, *"Hast thou eaten of the tree, whereof I commanded thee that thou shouldest not eat?"* (Genesis 3:11).

Obedience to God's command, which was the virtue of Paradise, included every good behavior God desires in His kingdom. It was the one condition of man's living there, the one thing his Creator asked of him.

The Blessings of Obedience

Adam and Eve disobeyed God by eating fruit from the Tree of Knowledge. Immediately they understood the difference between good and evil.

They knew their sin would anger God, so they hid themselves. Yet God knew they had disobeyed Him. He could not tolerate disobedience in Paradise: *"The LORD God sent him forth from the garden....he drove out the man"* (Genesis 3:23–24). God said nothing directly about faith, humility, or love because obedience includes all of these things. God's demand for obedience is as supreme as His authority. Obedience is the one thing necessary in man's life.

Restoring Our Obedience

God carries the theme of obedience throughout His Word. In Revelation 22:14, He says, *"Blessed are they that do his commandments, that they may have right to the tree of life."*

From beginning to end, from Paradise lost to Paradise regained, God's law is unchangeable. Only obedience gives man access to the Tree of Life and God's favor.

You may ask how man gained access to the Tree of Life when his original disobedience closed the way. Romans 5:19 describes the work done through the Cross of Christ: *"For as by one man's disobedience many were made sinners, so by the obedience of one shall many be made righteous."* (See also Philippians 2:8–9 and Hebrews 5:8–9.)

10

Obedience: Its Place in Scripture

The whole redemption of Christ consists of restoring obedience to its place. The beauty of His salvation is that He brings us back to the life of obedience, through which the creature can give the Creator the glory due Him. It is in this way that the creature can also receive the glory his Creator desires to give him.

Paradise, Calvary, and heaven all proclaim with one voice, "Child of God, the first and the last thing your God asks of you is simple, universal, unchanging obedience."

Old Testament Obedience

In the Old Testament, obedience always came into special prominence with any new beginning in the history of God's kingdom. Noah, the new father of the human race, acted *"according to all that God commanded him"* (Genesis 6:22). The Bible mentions Noah's obedience four times. God entrusts His work to the man who does what He commands. God will use the obedient man to save His people.

"By faith Abraham...obeyed" (Hebrews 11:8). God chose Abraham to be the father of the chosen race because He knew Abraham had an obedient heart. After Abraham had spent forty years learning faith and obedience, God came to perfect Abraham's faith and crown it with His fullest blessing. Nothing could prepare him for this but a supreme act of obedience. When Abraham had

11

The Blessings of Obedience

tied his son on the altar, God said, *"By myself have I sworn, saith the LORD...blessing I will bless thee, and...I will multiply thy seed....And in thy seed shall all the nations of the earth be blessed; because thou hast obeyed my voice."* (Genesis 22:16–18).

This blessing continued for Isaac: *"I will perform the oath which I sware unto Abraham....because that Abraham obeyed my voice"* (Genesis 26:3, 5). When will we learn how unspeakably pleasing obedience is in God's sight? When will we understand how great the reward is that He bestows because of obedience? To be a blessing to the world, be obedient. Let God and the world know you by this one characteristic—a will completely given up to God's will.

On Mount Sinai, God gave Moses this message: *"If ye will obey my voice indeed, and keep my covenant, then ye shall be a peculiar treasure unto me above all people"* (Exodus 19:5).

In the very nature of things, it cannot be otherwise. God's holy will is His glory and perfection. Only by entering His will through obedience is it possible to be His people. The Bible says nineteen times that Moses, while building the sanctuary where God was to dwell, acted *"according to all that the LORD commanded him"* (Exodus 40:16, for example). Because Moses obeyed God, *"the glory of the LORD filled the tabernacle"* (v. 34). *"The glory of the LORD appeared unto all the people. And there came a fire out from before*

Obedience: Its Place in Scripture

the LORD, and consumed upon the altar the burnt offering" (Leviticus 9:23–24).

God delights to dwell in the midst of His people's obedience. He crowns the obedient with His favor and presence.

After the forty years of wandering in the wilderness and its terrible revelation of the fruit of disobedience, the Hebrews were ready for a new beginning. They were about to enter Canaan. In describing the Hebrew nation at this time, the book of Deuteronomy uses the word *obey* and speaks of the blessing obedience brings more frequently than any other book. The whole idea is summed up in the words, *"I set before you....A blessing, if ye obey....And a curse, if ye will not obey."* (Deuteronomy 11:26–28).

Yes, a *"blessing, if ye obey"*! This is the keynote of the Christian life. Our Canaan, just like Paradise and heaven, is the place of blessing as well as the place of obedience. It would be wonderful if we could take it in! But beware of praying only for a blessing. Let us be concerned with obedience; God will take care of the blessing. Let your one thought as a Christian be how you can obey and please your God perfectly.

Obedience and the Kings of Israel

Obedience was crucial again in the appointment of kings in Israel. In the story of Saul, we have the solemn warning about the need for exact

The Blessings of Obedience

and entire obedience in a man whom God is to trust as ruler of His people. Samuel commanded Saul, *"Seven days shalt thou tarry, till I come to thee, and show thee what thou shalt"* (1 Samuel 10:8). When Samuel delayed, Saul took it upon himself to offer the sacrifice.

When Samuel finally came, he said, *"Thou hast done foolishly: thou hast not kept the commandment of the LORD thy God....now thy kingdom shall not continue....because thou hast not kept that which the LORD commanded thee"* (1 Samuel 13:13–14). God will not honor the man who is not obedient.

Saul had a second opportunity to show God what was in his heart. God sent him to execute judgment against Amalek. Saul obeyed. He gathered an army of 200,000 men, started the journey into the wilderness, and destroyed Amalek. But while God commanded him to *"utterly destroy all that they have, and spare them not"* (1 Samuel 15:3), Saul spared the best of the cattle and Agag.

God spoke to Samuel, saying, *"It repenteth me that I have set up Saul to be king: for he...hath not performed my commandments"* (v. 11).

When Samuel came, Saul said to him, *"I have performed the commandment of the LORD"* (v. 13); *"I have obeyed the voice of the LORD"* (v. 20).

He had obeyed, as many would think. But his obedience had not been entire. God claims exact, full obedience. God had said, *"Utterly destroy all...and spare them not"* (v. 3). Saul had not done this. He had spared the best sheep for a sacrifice to the Lord. And Samuel said, *"To obey is better than sacrifice....Because thou hast rejected the word of the LORD, he hath also rejected thee"* (vv. 22–23). There is no substitute for obedience.

Saul's partial obedience is sadly typical of contemporary obedience that performs God's commandment in part yet is not the obedience God desires! God says of all sin and disobedience, *"Utterly destroy all...and spare* [it] *not"* (v. 3). May God reveal to us whether we are indeed going all lengths with Him, seeking to destroy all sin, and sparing nothing within us that is not in perfect harmony with His will. It is only a wholehearted obedience, down to the smallest detail, that can satisfy God. Let nothing less satisfy you so that you will not say, "I have obeyed," while God says, *"Thou has rejected the word of the LORD"* (1 Samuel 15:26).

Benefits of Obedience

Jeremiah is also a book full of the word *obey,* though it contains complaints that the people had not obeyed God. God sums up all His dealings with the fathers in this passage: *"I spake not unto your fathers...concerning burnt offerings or sacrifices: But this thing commanded I them,*

The Blessings of Obedience

saying, Obey my voice, and I will be your God"
(Jeremiah 7:22–23).

We need to learn that sacrifices, even the sacrifice of God's beloved Son, are subordinate to one thing—restoring His creature to full obedience. You cannot enter God's blessing when He says, *"I will be your God,"* unless you first *"obey [His] voice."*

In the New Testament, we immediately think of our blessed Lord Jesus Christ and the importance He placed on obedience as the one reason He came into the world. Jesus entered the world saying, *"Lo, I come to do thy will, O God"* (Hebrews 10:9). He always confessed to men, *"I seek not mine own will, but the will of the Father which hath sent me"* (John 5:30). Of all He did and suffered, even to death, He said, *"This commandment have I received of my Father."* (John 10:18). In Christ's teaching, we find everywhere that He claims the same obedience He rendered to the Father from everyone who desires to be His disciple.

During His entire ministry, from beginning to end, He said obedience was the very essence of salvation. In the Sermon on the Mount, He began with this subject. No one could enter the kingdom *"but he that doeth the will of my Father which is in heaven"* (Matthew 7:21). In His farewell discourse, He wonderfully revealed the spiritual character of true obedience. It is born of love, is inspired by it, and opens the way into the

16

Obedience: Its Place in Scripture

love of God. Take into your heart these wonderful words:

> *If ye love me, keep my commandments. And...the Father...shall give you another Comforter, that he may abide with you for ever....He that hath my commandments, and keepeth them, he it is that loveth me: and he...shall be loved of my Father, and I will love him, and will manifest myself to him....If a man love me, he will keep my words: and my Father will love him, and we will come unto him, and make our abode with him.*
> (John 14:15–16, 21, 23)

No words could express more simply or more powerfully the glorious place Christ gives to obedience. It is only possible with a loving heart. Obedience opens the door to all that God has to give of His Holy Spirit, His wonderful love, and His indwelling in Christ Jesus. No Scripture passage gives a higher revelation of the spiritual life or the power of loving obedience than John 14. Let us pray and earnestly ask God that, by His Holy Spirit, light may transfigure our daily obedience with its heavenly glory.

Living Daily in His Commandments

The next chapter of John's gospel, the parable of the Vine, confirms this idea. How often and earnestly we have asked to be able to live continually like Christ! We think that studying the Word, having more faith, offering more prayer, or attaining more communion with God will make us Christlike. Yet we have overlooked one simple truth. Jesus clearly teaches, *"If ye keep my commandments, ye shall abide in my love; even as I have kept my Father's commandments, and abide in his love"* (John 15:10).

For Him, as for us, the only way under heaven to live in divine love is to keep the commandments. Have you known obedience? Have you heard it preached? Have you believed it and proved it true in your experience that obedience on earth is the key to a place in God's love in heaven? Unless there is some correspondence between God's wholehearted love in heaven and our wholehearted, loving obedience on earth, Christ cannot manifest Himself to us. God cannot abide in us. We cannot live in His love.

In the book of Acts, Peter showed how our Lord's teaching entered into him. He said it was by *"the Holy Ghost, whom God hath given to them that obey him"* (Acts 5:32). He showed that the preparation for Pentecost was surrender to Christ. He also said, *"We ought to obey God rather than men"* (v. 29). We are to be obedient, even unto death. Nothing on earth can dare to hinder obedience in the man who has given himself to God.

In Paul's epistle to the Romans, he asserted, in the opening and closing verses, that *"obedience to the faith among all nations"* (Romans 1:5; see 16:26) was the reason he had been made an apostle. He spoke of what God made happen *"to make the Gentiles obedient"* (Romans 15:18). He taught that, as the obedience of Christ makes us righteous, we become the servants of obedience. As disobedience in Adam and in us was what brought death, so obedience in Christ and in us is the one thing that the Gospel makes known as the way of restoration to God and His favor.

Listening to and Obeying the Word

James warned us, *"But be ye doers of the word, and not hearers only, deceiving your own selves"* (James 1:22). He then described how Abraham was justified and his faith was perfected by his works.

In Peter's first epistle, obedience has an important place in his system. In 1 Peter 1:2, he spoke to the *"elect...through sanctification of the Spirit, unto obedience and sprinkling of the blood of Jesus Christ."* He showed us that obedience is the eternal purpose of the Father. It is the great objective of the work of the Spirit and a chief part of the salvation of Christ. He wrote, *"As obedient children....so be ye holy in all manner of conversation"* (vv. 14–15).

Obedience is the starting point of true holiness. Later on we read, *"Seeing ye have purified your souls in obeying the truth"* (v. 22). Complete acceptance of God's truth is not merely a matter of intellectual assent or strong emotion. It is

The Blessings of Obedience

subjecting one's life to the dominion of the truth of God. The Christian life is, first and foremost, characterized by obedience.

We know how strong John's statements are. *"He that saith, I know him, and keepeth not his commandments, is a liar, and the truth is not in him."* (1 John 2:4). Obedience is the certificate of Christian character.

> *Let us...love...in deed and in truth. And hereby we...shall assure our hearts before him....And whatsoever we ask, we receive of him, because we keep his commandments, and do those things that are pleasing in his sight.* (1 John 3:18–19, 22)

Is God Listening to You?

Obedience is the secret of a good conscience and the confidence that God hears us. *"This is the love of God, that we keep his commandments"* (1 John 5:3). We reveal our love for God, to Him as well as to the world, through our cheerful obedience.

Obedience holds this high place in Scripture, in the mind of God, and in the hearts of His servants. We should ask ourselves if it takes that place in our hearts and lives. Have we given obedience the supreme place of authority over ourselves that God intends it to have? Is it the inspiration of every action and every approach to Him?

Obedience: Its Place in Scripture

If we yield ourselves to the searching of God's Spirit, we may find that we never gave obedience its proper proportion in our scheme of life and that this lack is the cause of all our failure in prayer and in work. We may see that the deeper blessings of God's grace, and the full enjoyment of God's love and nearness, have been beyond our reach simply because we never made obedience what God intended it to be. It is the starting point and the goal of our Christian lives.

Let this, our first study, awaken in us an earnest desire to fully know God's will concerning this truth. Let us unite in prayer that the Holy Spirit will show us how defective the Christian's life is when obedience does not rule everything. Let Him show us how that life can be exchanged for one of full surrender and absolute obedience. We can then be sure that God in Christ will enable us to live this life successfully.

Chapter Two

Christ's Obedience

*"So by the obedience of one shall
many be made righteous."*
—Romans 5:19

*"Know ye not, that...servants ye are to...
obedience unto righteousness?"*
—Romans 6:16

Through the obedience of One, many will be made righteous. These words tell us what we owe Christ. In Adam, we were made sinners; in Christ, we are made righteous.

The words also tell us that we owe our righteousness to the obedience of Christ. Among the treasures of our inheritance in Christ, this is one of the richest. Many people have never studied the blessing of obedience so as to love it, delight in it, and receive the full benefit of it. May God by

23

The Blessings of Obedience

His Holy Spirit reveal the glory of obedience and make us partakers of its power.

You are most likely familiar with the blessed truth of justification by faith. From Romans 3:21 to 5:11, Paul taught that the foundation of our justification was the atonement of the blood of Christ. He taught that the way to receive it is by faith in the free grace of God, who *"justifieth the ungodly"* (Romans 4:5). The blessed fruit of justification is the bestowal of Christ's righteousness, immediate access into God's favor, and the hope of future glory.

In Romans 5:19, where we read that *"by the obedience of one shall many be made righteous"* Paul discussed our union with Adam and all the consequences that flow from that union. He proved how reasonable it is that those who receive Christ by faith, and are then united with Him, share His life and His righteousness in God's eyes. In this argument, Paul emphasized the contrast between Adam's disobedience, with the condemnation and death it brought, and Christ's obedience, with the goodness and life it brought.

The Twofold Connection

"By one man's disobedience many were made sinners" (Romans 5:19). How was this?

There was a twofold connection between Adam and his descendants: the judicial and the inherited. Through the judicial, the whole race, though unborn, was immediately under the sentence of death. *"Death reigned from Adam to Moses, even over them that had not sinned after the similitude of Adam's transgression"* (v. 14). This even included little children.

This judicial relationship was rooted in the inherited connection. The sentence could not have come upon them if they had not been descendants of Adam. Each child of Adam enters life under the power of sin and death. Through the disobedience of one, *"many were made sinners"* (v. 19). We were all subject to the curse of sin; and by nature, we were subject to sin's power.

"Adam…is the figure of him that was to come" (v. 14). Jesus, who is called the Second Adam, is the second Father of the race. The effects of Adam's disobedience are exactly parallel to those of Christ's obedience. When a sinner believes in Jesus Christ, he is united to Him. Immediately by a judicial sentence, the believer is accepted as conforming to God's will—in God's sight. The judicial relationship is rooted in the physical.

Man has Christ's righteousness only by believing his sins are forgiven because of Christ's sacrifice. Before a saved person understands any of the fine points about living for Jesus, he can rest assured that he is acquitted and accepted. The believer is then led on to know that, as real and complete as was his participation in Adam's disobedience, so also is his participation in Christ's obedience real. He now enjoys both the righteousness and the obedient life and nature that comes from it.

A Deeper Look

Through Adam's disobedience, we were made sinners. The one thing God asked of Adam in Paradise was obedience. The one thing by which a creature can glorify God or enjoy His favor and blessing is obedience.

Sin has power in the world because of disobedience. The entire curse of sin is due to disobedience imputed to us. The power of sin working in us is nothing but Adam's nature. We have inherited his disobedience. We are born *the children of disobedience* (Ephesians 2:2).

It is evident that Christ needed to remove this disobedience—its curse, its dominion, its evil nature and workings. Disobedience is the root of all sin and misery. The first goal of His salvation was to cut away the evil root and restore man to his original destiny: a life of obedience to his God. How did Christ do this?

First, He did this by coming as the Second Adam to undo what the First Adam had done. Sin made us believe it was humiliating to continually be seeking to know and do God's will. Christ came to show us the nobility, the blessedness, and the delight of obedience. When God gave us the robe of creaturehood to wear, we did not know that its beauty and unspotted purity was from obedience to God. Christ came, put on that robe, and showed us how to wear it. He showed us how we could enter into the presence and glory of God. Christ came to overcome, take away our disobedience, and replace it with His own obedience. As universal, as mighty, as all-pervading as was the disobedience of Adam, far more pervasive was the power of Christ's obedience.

Christ's Three-Part Goal

The purpose of Christ's life of obedience was threefold. First, He came to be an example of true obedience. Second, He came to be our surety, to fulfill all righteousness for us by His obedience. Finally, He came to be our Head, to prepare a new and obedient nature in us.

He also died to show us that His obedience meant a readiness to obey to the uttermost, to die for God. Obedience is the vicarious endurance and atonement of the guilt of our disobedience. It means a death to sin as an entrance into the life of God for Him and for us.

The disobedience of Adam and all of its repercussions were to be put away and replaced by the obedience of Christ. Judicially, by that obedience, we are made righteous. Just as we were made sinners by Adam's disobedience, we are immediately and completely justified and delivered from the power of sin and death. We stand before God as righteous men and women in Christ. The life we receive in Him is a life of obedience.

Everyone who desires to understand obedience should consider this well. Obeying Christ is the secret of conforming to God's will and the salvation one finds in Him. Obedience is the very essence of that righteousness. Obedience is salvation. The obedience of Jesus should be accepted, trusted, and rejoiced in as covering, swallowing up, and ending disobedience. Jesus Christ's obedience to God is the one unchanging, never-to-be-forsaken basis of my acceptance. And then, His obedience becomes the life power of the new nature in me, just as Adam's disobedience was the power of death that ruled my life.

If by one man's offence death reigned by one; much more they which receive abundance of grace and of the gift of righteousness shall reign in life by one, Jesus Christ....the free gift came upon all men unto justification of life. (Romans 5:17–18)

As we examine the significance of the First and Second Adam, we see the parallel between death and disobedience, and life and obedience. We cannot escape being inheritors of Adam's death through his disobedience. In the same way, when we believe in Jesus Christ, we are equally inseparable from His obedience and life. We have His obedience by association as well as for our personal possession. By accepting the atoning work of Christ's blood, we exchange our death inheritance for His life inheritance.

Discussion in Romans

Paul drew this connection in Romans 6:12–13 for the first time in his letter. Paul directed the Roman church, *"Let not sin therefore reign...Yield yourselves unto God."* Then he immediately proceeded to teach how this means nothing but obedience: *"Know ye not, that...ye are* [servants] *to whom ye obey; whether of sin unto death, or of obedience unto righteousness?"* (v. 16).

Our relationship to obedience is a practical one. We have been delivered from disobedience (Adam's and our own), and now we are servants of obedience *"unto righteousness."* Christ's obedience was righteousness—God's gift to us. Our subjection to obedience is the only way we can maintain our relationship to God and righteousness. Christ's obedience, which gained us righteousness, is only the beginning of life for us. Our conforming to God's will is the only way to continue life.

One Law

There is only one law for the Head and the members. As surely as this law was disobedience and death for Adam and his seed, it is obedience and life for Christ and His seed. The one bond of union, the one likeness between Adam and his seed, was disobedience. The resemblance between Christ and His seed is obedience.

Obedience alone made Christ the object of the Father's love and, as a result, our Redeemer.

> *Therefore doth my Father love me, because I lay down my life, that I might take it again. No man taketh it from me, but I lay it down of myself. I have power to lay it down, and I have power to take it again. This commandment have I received of my Father.*
> (John 10:17–18)

Only obedience can lead us to dwell in that love and enjoy that redemption.

> *He that hath my commandments, and keepeth them, he it is that loveth me: and he that loveth me shall be loved of my Father, and I will love him, and will manifest myself to him....If a man love me, he will keep my words: and my Father will love him, and we will come unto him, and make our abode with him.*
> (John 14:21, 23)

Everything depends on our knowledge of and participation in obedience. Obedience is the gateway and path to the full enjoyment of a right relationship to God. At conversion, righteousness is given because of faith—once, completely, and forever. We receive righteousness even though we have little or no knowledge of obedience. But as the Christian believes he is in God's favor,

Christ's Obedience

submits to God's will, and seeks to be a servant of righteousness, this sanctification in God's eyes will pour blessing on him and lead back to its divine origin. The stronger our hold of the righteousness of Christ in the power to the Spirit, the more intense our desire will be to share in the obedience out of which it came.

Principles of Christ's Obedience

Studying the following principles of Christ's obedience will help us to live as servants of obedience who desire a right relationship with God. In Christ, this obedience was a life principle. Obedience with Him did not mean a single act of obedience now and then, or even a series of acts, but the spirit of His whole life. *"I came...not to do mine own will"* (John 6:38). *"Lo, I come to do thy will, O God"* (Hebrews 10:9). Jesus came into the world for one purpose. He lived only to carry out God's will. The single, supreme, all-controlling power of His life was obedience.

Jesus is willing to make us able to do the same. This was what He promised when He said, *"For whosoever shall do the will of my Father which is in heaven, the same is my brother, and sister, and mother"* (Matthew 12:50).

The link in a family is a common life shared by all and a family likeness. The bond between Christ and us is that together we do the will of God.

The Blessings of Obedience

For Christ, this obedience was a joy. *"I delight to do thy will, O my God"* (Psalm 40:8). *"My meat is to do the will of him that sent me"* (John 4:34).

Our food is refreshment and invigoration. The healthy man eats his bread with pleasure. But food is more than enjoyment; it is a necessity of life. Likewise, doing the will of God was the food that Christ hungered after; without this, He could not live. Obedience was the one thing that satisfied His hunger, the one thing that refreshed Him, strengthened Him, and made Him happy.

This was David's idea when he spoke of God's Word being *"sweeter...than honey and the honeycomb"* (Psalm 19:10). As this is understood and accepted, obedience will become more natural and necessary for us. It will become more refreshing than our daily food.

For Christ, this obedience led to His waiting for God to reveal His will.

God did not reveal all His will to Christ at once, but day by day, according to the circumstances of the hour. In His life of obedience, there was growth and progress; the most difficult lesson was the last. Each act of obedience equipped Him for the new discovery of the Father's next command. He spoke, *"Mine ears hast thou opened....I delight to do thy will, O my God"* (Psalm 40:6, 8).

As obedience becomes the fervor of our lives, God's Spirit will open our ears to wait for His teaching. We will be content with nothing less than divine guidance into God's perfect will for us.

In Christ, this obedience was unto death.

When He spoke, *"I came down from heaven, not to do mine own will, but the will of him that sent me"* (John 6:38), He was ready to go to all lengths in denying His own will and doing the Father's will. He may have said to Himself, "In nothing, My will; at all costs, God's will."

This is the obedience to which He invites us and for which He empowers us. This wholehearted surrender to obedience in everything is the only true obedience. It is the only power that will survive to carry us through life. If only Christians could understand that nothing less than obedience brings joy and strength to the soul!

As long as there is a doubt about universal obedience, and with that a lurking sense of the possibility of failure, we lose the confidence that secures the victory. But when we recognize that God is asking for full obedience, we must then decide to work at it and offer Him nothing less. If we give ourselves up to the working of the divine power, the Holy Spirit can master our entire lives.

In Christ, this obedience sprang from the deepest humility. *"Let this mind be in you, which was also in Christ Jesus: Who...made himself of no reputation, and took upon him the form of a servant, and...humbled himself, and became obedient unto death"* (Philippians 2:5–8).

The Blessings of Obedience

It is the man who is willing to entirely empty himself, to be and to live as a servant of obedience, to be humbled before God and man, to whom the obedience of Jesus will unfold its heavenly beauty and power. He may have a strong will that secretly trusts in self, that strives for obedience and fails. Only as we approach God in humility, meekness, patience, and entire resignation to His will does He reveal to us the blessings in obedience. To see this blessing in our duty, we must bow in absolute helplessness and dependence on Him, turning away wholly from self.

In Christ, this obedience was faith in entire dependence upon God's strength. *"I can of mine own self do nothing"* (John 5:30). *"The Father that dwelleth in me, he doeth the works"* (John 14:10).

The Son's unreserved surrender to the Father's will was met by the Father's unceasing and unreserved bestowal of His power working in Him.

God's Power—Our Obedience

It will be even so with us. If we learn that giving up our wills to God is always the measure of His giving His power to us, we will see that a surrender to full obedience is nothing but a full faith that God will work all in us.

God's promises of the new covenant all rest on this Scripture: *"And the LORD thy God will*

Christ's Obedience

*circumcise thine heart...to love the LORD thy God
with all thine heart....And thou shalt return and
obey the voice of the LORD"* (Deuteronomy 30:6,
8–9). *"I will put my spirit within you, and cause
you to walk in my statutes, and ye shall keep my
judgments, and do them"* (Ezekiel 36:27).

Let us, like the Son, believe that God works
everything in us, and we will have the courage
to yield ourselves to an unreserved obedience, an
obedience unto death. This yielding ourselves up
to God will become the entrance into the blessed
experience of conformity to the Son of God in
His doing the Father's will because He counted
on the Father's power. Let us give ourselves completely to God. He will work His entire work in
us.

Do you know that because you were made
righteous by the obedience of Jesus, you are like
Him? In Him you are servants of obedience,
growing more and more consistent with God's
nature. It is in the obedience of the One that
the obedience of the many has its root, its life,
and its security. Make it a point to study Christ
and believe in Him as the Obedient One. Seek,
receive, and love Him as the One to conform
yourself to. As His righteousness is our one hope,
let His obedience be our one desire.

Let us prove our sincerity and confidence
in God's supernatural power by accepting Jesus
Christ as the Obedient One, the Christ who dwells
in us.

Chapter Three

Christ's School of Obedience

*"Though he were a Son, yet learned
he obedience."*
—Hebrews 5:8

The secret of true obedience is a close and unmistakable personal relationship with God. All our attempts to be fully obedient will be failures until we gain access to His abiding fellowship. It is God's holy presence consciously abiding with us that keeps us from disobeying Him.

Defective obedience is always the result of a defective life. To rouse and spur on that defective life by arguments and motives has its use. The chief blessing of the arguments must be that they make us feel the need for a different life, a life so entirely under the power of God that obedience will be natural.

The Blessings of Obedience

The defective life, the life of broken and irregular fellowship with God, must be healed to make way for a full and healthy life. Then, full obedience will become possible. The secret of true obedience is the return to close and continual fellowship with God.

The Necessity of Obedience

"He learned obedience." Why was this necessary for Christ? What is the blessing He brings us? *Though he were a Son, yet learned he obedience by the things which he suffered; And...became the author of eternal salvation unto all them that obey him"* (Hebrews 5:8–9).

Suffering is unnatural to us and therefore calls for the surrender of our wills.

Christ needed to suffer so that He could learn to obey and give up His will to the Father at any cost. He needed to learn obedience so that, as our great High Priest, He would be made perfect. "He learned obedience." He became obedient even to death so that He could become the Author of our salvation. As the Author of salvation through obedience, He now saves those who obey Him.

The very essence of salvation is obedience to God. Christ as the Obedient One saves us as His obedient ones. Whether in His suffering on earth or in His glory in heaven, Christ's heart is set on obedience.

Christ's School of Obedience

On earth, Christ learned in the school of obedience. From heaven, He teaches obedience to His disciples here on earth. In a world where disobedience reigns for death, the restoration of obedience is in Christ's hands. As in His own life, so in us; He has made a contract to maintain obedience in us. He teaches us and works it in us.

Think about what and how He teaches. When we think of an ordinary school, we usually ask about the teacher, the textbooks, and the students. Let us examine these things regarding Christ's school of obedience. It may be we will see how little we have devoted ourselves to learning obedience and only obedience.

The Teacher

"He learned obedience." Now Jesus teaches us by unfolding the secret of His own obedience to the Father.

I have said that we find the power of true obedience in our personal relationship with God. It was the same with our Lord Jesus. Of all His teaching, He said,

> For I have not spoken of myself; but the Father which sent me, he gave me a commandment, what I should say, and what I should speak. And I know that his commandment is life everlasting: whatsoever I speak therefore, even as the Father said unto me, so I speak.
> (John 12:49–50)

The Blessings of Obedience

This does not mean that Christ received God's commandment in eternity as part of the Father's commission to Him on entering the world. No. Day by day, as He taught and worked, He lived in continual communication with the Father. He received the Father's instructions as He needed them.

He even said,

> *The Son can do nothing of himself, but what he seeth the Father do....For the Father...showeth him all things that himself doeth: and he will show him greater works than these....as I hear, I judge....for I am not alone, but I and the Father that sent me....but the Father that dwelleth in me.*
> (John 5:19–20, 30; 8:16; 14:10)

Obedience is constant dependence on a moment-by-moment fellowship and operation of God, a hearing and seeing of what God speaks, does, and shows.

Our Lord always spoke of His relationship with the Father as parallel to our relationship with Him and with the Father through Him. This parallel relationship also carried the same promise. With us, as with Jesus, the life of continual obedience is impossible without continual fellowship and teaching. We must believe in God's power and receive Him into our lives. We must believe His presence is eternal, the same way Jesus believed. Only then will we have any hope of bringing every thought into captivity—into Christlike obedience (2 Corinthians 10:5).

The absolute necessity of continually receiving our orders and instructions from God Himself is what the Bible implies when it says, *"Obey my voice, and I will be your God"* (Jeremiah 7:23).

The expression "obeying the commandments" is seldom used in Scripture. God usually says, "obeying Me" or "obeying (or hearkening to) My voice." The army commander, the school teacher, and the head of a family do not win obedience through a code of laws, rewards, or threats. Their personal living awakens love and enthusiasm. It is the joy of hearing the Father's voice that will provide the joy and strength of true obedience. God's voice gives power to obey the Word; the Word without His living voice brings no profit.

The Bible contrasts this principle with what we see in Israel. The people had heard the voice of God on Mount Sinai and were afraid. They asked Moses to ask God not to speak to them. They wanted Moses to receive the Word of God and bring it to them. The Israelites thought only of the command. They did not know that the only power to obey is in the presence of God and His voice speaking to us. With only Moses and the tablets of stone to speak to them, their whole history is one of disobedience because they were afraid of direct contact with God.

Christians are often the same way today. Many Christians find it much easier to take their

The Blessings of Obedience

teaching from godly men than to serve God and receive it directly from Him. Their faith stands in the wisdom of men and not in the power of God. (See 1 Corinthians 2:5.)

Learn the great lesson from our Lord, who learned obedience by waiting, moment by moment, to see and hear what the Father had to teach. It is only when, like Jesus and through Him, we always walk with God and hear His voice, that we can possibly attempt to offer God the obedience He asks for and promises to work in us.

Out of the depths of His own life and experience, Christ can give and teach us obedience. Pray earnestly that God will show you the foolishness of attempting to obey without the same strength Christ needed. Pray that He will make you willing to give up everything for the Christlike joy of the Father's constant presence.

The Textbook

Christ's direct communication with the Father did not make Him independent of Scripture. In the divine school of obedience, there is only one textbook, whether for our Older Brother, Jesus, or the younger children. While He learned obedience, He used the same textbook we have. He needed the Word and used it for His own special life and guidance as well as for teaching and convincing others.

Christ's School of Obedience

From the beginning of His public life to its close, He lived by the Word of God. *"It is written"* was the sword of the Spirit with which He conquered Satan (Matthew 4:4, 7, 10). *"The Spirit of the LORD is upon me"* (Luke 4:18). This word of Scripture was the frame of reference with which He opened His Gospel preaching.

"That the scripture might be fulfilled" (John 17:12) was the light in which He accepted all suffering and even gave Himself to the death. After the Resurrection, He expounded to the disciples *"in all the scriptures the things concerning himself"* (Luke 24:27).

In Scripture, He found God's plan and path marked out for Him. He gave Himself to fulfill it. It was in and with the use of God's Word that He received the Father's continual, direct teaching.

In God's school of obedience, the Bible is the only textbook. This fact shows us the attitude in which we are to come to the Bible. We are to come with the simple desire to find God's will concerning us, and then we are to do it.

Scripture was not written to increase our knowledge. It was written to guide our conduct, *"That the man of God may be perfect, thoroughly furnished unto all good works"* (2 Timothy 3:17). *"If any man will do his will, he shall know of the doctrine, whether it be of God, or whether I speak of myself"* (John 7:17).

The Blessings of Obedience

Learn from Christ's example that God's goal is for man to be prepared to do His will as it is done in heaven. He desires man to be restored to perfect obedience and its blessings. The scriptural revelation of God, His love, and His counsel are secondary to His main goal.

In God's school of obedience, His Word is the only textbook. To apply that Word in His own life and conduct, to know when each portion was to be taken up and carried out, Christ needed and received divine instruction. Jesus Christ spoke in Isaiah, *"The Lord GOD...wakeneth* [me] *morning by morning, he wakeneth mine ear to hear as the learned. The Lord GOD hath opened mine ear"* (Isaiah 50:4–5).

Jesus teaches us in this same way by giving us the Holy Spirit as the divine Interpreter of the Word. This is the great work of the indwelling Holy Spirit. The Word we read, He plants in our hearts. He coaches us to think about it. It then works effectively in our wills, our love, and our whole beings. When we do not understand this, the Word has no power to help us in obedience.

Speaking plainly about this, we rejoice in the increased attention given to Bible study, and in testimonies about the benefit received. But let's not deceive ourselves. We may delight in studying the Bible. We may admire and be charmed with the views we see of God's truth. The thoughts suggested may make a deep impression and awaken the most pleasing religious emotions. Yet the practical influence in making us holy, humble, loving, patient, and ready, either for service or suffering, may be very small. The one reason for this is that we do not receive the Word as the Word of a living God who must speak to us Himself in order for its divine power to be exerted.

The letter of the Word, however we study and delight in it, has no saving or sanctifying power. Human wisdom and human will, however strenuous their effort, cannot give or command that power. The Holy Spirit is the mighty power of God. It is only as the Holy Spirit teaches you, only as the Gospel is preached to you by man or book, *"with the Holy Ghost sent down from heaven"* (1 Peter 1:12), that it will really give you the strength to obey the very thing commanded.

With man, knowing, doing, willing, and performing are, for lack of power, often separate and even at opposite poles. This is never so in the Holy Spirit. He is at once the light and the might of God. All He is, does, and gives has the truth and the power of God in it equally. When He shows you God's command, He always shows it to you as a possible and a certain thing. He shows it to you as a divine life, a gift prepared for you, which He is able to give.

Beloved, learn to believe that it is only when Christ, through the Holy Spirit, teaches you to understand and take the Word into your hearts that He can really teach you to obey the Father as He did. Believe, every time you open your

Bible, that just as sure as you listen to the divine, Spirit-breathed Word, your Father will, in answer to the prayer of faith, give the Holy Spirit's living operation in your hearts.

Let all your Bible study be done in faith. Do not simply try to believe the truths or promises you read. Your faith may then be in your own power. Believe in the Holy Spirit, in His being in you, and in God's working in you through Him. Take the Word into your hearts in the quiet faith that He will enable you to love it, yield to it, and keep it. Believe that our blessed Lord Jesus will make the Bible mean to you what it meant to Him when He spoke of *"the things* [that are written] *concerning Himself"* (Luke 24:27). Scripture will become the simple revelation of what God is going to do for you, in you, and through you.

The Student

We have seen how our Lord teaches us obedience by unfolding the secret of His learning it. He shows us His unceasing dependence on the Father. We have seen how He teaches us to use the sacred Book as He used it, as a divine revelation of what God has ordained for us.

He has given us the Holy Spirit to expound and enforce the Word in us. If we now consider the place the believer takes in the school of obedience as a student, we will better understand what

Christ the Son requires in order to do His work in us effectively.

In a faithful student, there are several things that make up his feelings toward a trusted teacher. He submits himself entirely to his instructor's leading. He has perfect trust in him. He gives the teacher just as much time and attention as he asks.

When we see and consent that Jesus Christ has a right to all this, we can hope to experience how wonderfully He can teach us an obedience like His own. The good student, great musicians and painters say, yields his master a wholehearted and unhesitating submission. In practicing scales or mixing colors, in the slow and patient study of the elements of art, the student knows that it is wise to simply and fully obey his teacher.

It is this wholehearted surrender to His guidance, this implicit submission to His authority, that Christ asks. We come to Him, asking Him to teach us the lost art of obeying God as He did. He asks us if we are ready to pay the price. The price is to entirely deny self! It is to give up our wills and our lives to the death! It is to be ready to do whatever He says!

The only way to learn to do something is to do it. The only way to learn obedience from Christ is to give up our wills to Him and make doing His will the one desire and delight of our hearts.

The Blessings of Obedience

Unless you take the vow of absolute obedience as you enter this class of Christ's school, it will be impossible for you to make any progress.

The true scholar of a great master finds it easy to render him this implicit obedience, simply because he trusts his teacher. He gladly sacrifices his own wisdom and will in order to be guided by a higher authority.

We need this confidence in our Lord Jesus. He came from heaven to learn obedience and be able to teach it well. His obedience is the treasury out of which the debt of our past is paid and the grace for our present obedience is supplied. In His divine love and perfect human sympathy, in His divine power over our hearts and lives, He invites, He deserves, and He wins our trust.

Jesus touches us through our attachment to and admiration of Him. Through the power of His divine love, His Holy Spirit awakens within us a responsive love. Jesus then awakens our confidence and communicates to us the secret of true success.

As absolutely as we have trusted Him as our Savior who atoned for our disobedience, we can trust Him as a teacher to lead us out of it. Christ is our prophet and teacher. A heart that enthusiastically believes in His power and success as a teacher will, in the joy of that faith, find it easy to obey God. It is Christ's presence with us all day that will be our key to true obedience.

Christ's School of Obedience

A scholar gives his master just as much of his attendance and attention as he asks. The master determines how much time must be devoted to personal fellowship and instruction.

Obedience to God is a heavenly art. Our human nature is so utterly unfamiliar with it. We must not doubt if obedience does not come all at once, since the path in which the Son Himself learned it was slow and long. Nor must we wonder if we need to spend more time than most believers are ready to give waiting in prayer, meditation, and dependent self-sacrifice. Simply give it.

In Christ Jesus, heavenly obedience has become human again. Obedience has become our birthright and our life breath. Let us cling to our Lord; let us believe and claim His abiding presence. With Jesus Christ who learned obedience as our Savior, and who teaches obedience as our Master, we can live lives of obedience. We cannot study His lesson too seriously. His obedience is our salvation. In Him, the living Christ, we find obedience and partake of it moment by moment.

We must pray to God, asking Him to show us how Christ and His obedience are to be part of our daily lives. We must ask that He will then make us pupils who give Him all of our hearts and all of our time. He will teach us to keep His commandments and live in His love, even as He kept His Father's commandments and lives in His love.

Chapter Four

Morning Prayer

"For if the firstfruit be holy, the lump is also holy: and if the root be holy, so are the branches."
—Romans 11:16

The first day of the week, the holy day of rest, is a wonderful blessing from God. It is not that we have one day of rest and spiritual refreshment in the weariness of life; but this holy day, at the beginning of the week, can sanctify the whole. It will help us and prepare us to carry God's holy presence into the entire week and its work. With the first fruit holy, the entire lump is holy. With the root holy, all the branches are holy, too.

The Old Testament gives many types and examples of God providing power over temptation throughout the day as a result of a morning hour of prayer. The unspeakably gracious bond formed in that morning hour unites us with God and can be so firmly tied that when we have to live in the

The Blessings of Obedience

rush of men and duties, and we can scarcely think of God, our souls are kept safe and pure. The soul can so completely give itself into God's keeping during the time of secret worship that temptation only unites it closer with God. What cause for praise and joy, that the morning prayer can renew and strengthen our surrender to Jesus and faith in Him! The life of obedience can be maintained in fresh vigor and continue *"from strength to strength"* (Psalm 84:7).

The connection between obedience and morning prayer is intimate and vital. The desire for a life of entire obedience will give new meaning and value to our morning prayer, because this alone gives the strength and courage we need daily.

If we see prayer simply as a duty and a necessary part of our religious life, it will soon become a burden. Or if we pray thinking of our own happiness and safety, prayer will not be truly attractive. Only one thing will do—the desire for fellowship with God.

This is the reason we were created in God's likeness. Only living in His likeness can prepare us for a true and blessed life, either here or in heaven. He invites us to enter His inner chambers to know Him better, to receive His communication of love and strength, and to have our lives filled with His. It is in private, in morning prayer, that our spiritual lives are both tested and strengthened. That is the battlefield where it is decided whether we will give God absolute obedience. If we truly conquer there, giving ourselves into the hands of our almighty Lord, the victory during the day is certain. It is in the inner chamber where we prove whether we really delight in God and aim to love Him with our whole hearts.

Our first lesson is that the presence of God must be the chief thing in our devotions. When we learn that the purpose behind our morning prayer is to find His blessing, we will learn to long for it and delight in it. We will cherish meeting God, giving ourselves into His holy will, knowing we are pleasing Him, having Him lay His hands upon us, blessing us, and giving us our instructions. He then says, *"Go in this thy might"* (Judges 6:14).

Reading the Bible

Reading God's Word is part of our morning prayer time. I have several things I wish to say about this. Unless we are careful, the Word that is meant to point us to God may actually intervene and hide Him from us.

The mind may be occupied, interested, and delighted at what it finds. Yet because this is more head knowledge than anything else, it may bring us little good. If it does not lead us to wait on God, glorify Him, receive His grace and power for sweetening and sanctifying our lives, our reading becomes a hindrance instead of a help.

Another lesson that I cannot repeat too often is that it is only by the Holy Spirit's teaching that we can get at the real meaning of God's Word, and that the Word will really reach into our inner lives and work in us.

Our Father in heaven, who gave us His Word from heaven with its divine mysteries and message, also put His Holy Spirit in us to explain that Word and to allow us to take hold of it. The Father wants us to ask His Holy Spirit for teaching each time. He wants us to bow in a meek, teachable frame of mind and believe that the Spirit will, in the hidden depths of our hearts, make His Word live and work. He wants us to remember that He gave us the Spirit so that we would be led by Him, walk after Him, and have our whole lives under His rule. Therefore, He cannot teach us in the morning unless we honestly give ourselves up to His leading. But if we do this—wait patiently for Him, and serve Him, not to receive new thoughts, but to receive the power of the Word in our hearts—we can count on His teaching.

Let your closet be the classroom. Let your morning prayer be the study hour when you prove your relationship of entire dependence on and submission to the Holy Spirit's teaching.

Third, I want to confirm what was said above. Always study God's Word in the spirit of an unreserved surrender to obey. You know how often Christ and His apostles, in their epistles, spoke of hearing God's Word and not doing it.

Morning Prayer

If you accustom yourself to studying the Bible without an earnest and very definite purpose to obey, you will harden yourself in disobedience.

Never read God's will concerning you without honestly giving yourself up to do it immediately.

Ask for grace to do it. God gave us His Word to tell us what He wants us to do and how He provides His grace to enable us to do it. How sad to think it a pious thing just to read the Bible without any sincere effort to obey it! May God keep us from this terrible sin!

Let us make it a sacred habit to tell God, "Lord, whatever I know to be Your will, I will immediately obey." Always read with a heart yielded in willing obedience.

Finally, I have spoken of the commands we already know, and those that are easily understood. But remember, there are many commands that you may never have noticed, and others whose application is so wide and unceasing that you have not taken them in. Read God's Word with a deep desire to know all of His will. If there are things that appear difficult, commands that seem too hard, commands for which you need divine guidance to carry out, let them drive you to seek a divine teaching. It is not the text that is easiest and most encouraging that brings the most blessing. It is the text, whether easy or difficult, that throws you most upon God that brings the greatest blessing. God wants you to be *"filled with the knowledge of his will in all wisdom and spiritual understanding"* (Colossians 1:9). It is in the prayer closet where this wonderful work is to be done. Remember, it is only when you *know* God is telling you to do something that you feel sure He gives the strength to do it. It is only as we are willing to know all of God's will that He, from time to time, will reveal more of it to us, and that we will be able to do it all.

What a power the morning prayer time may be in the life of one who is determined to meet God daily! The person who renews his surrender to absolute obedience, and humbly and patiently waits on the Holy Spirit to teach God's will, is certain to find that every assurance and promise given in the Word is true.

Communion with God

In light of these thoughts, I would like to say a few words about what prayer should be in the morning prayer time.

First, secure the presence of God. Do not be content with anything less than having the assurance that God is looking at you in love, listening to you, and working in you.

If our daily lives are to be full of God, we need our morning prayer time where the life of the day can have God's seal stamped on it. In our religion, we need more of God—His love, His will, His holiness, His Spirit living in us, and His power working in us for our fellowmen. Under heaven there is no way of getting this except by close personal communion with Him. There is no better time for securing and practicing our communion with God than our morning prayer time.

The superficiality and feebleness of our religion and religious work all come from having little real contact with God. Since it is true that God alone is the foundation of all love and good and happiness, then our trust and highest happiness must be in Him. We desire to have in Him, as much as possible, His presence, His fellowship, His will, and the opportunity to serve Him. All of this being true, meeting God in morning prayer ought to be our first priority.

To have God appear to them and speak was the secret behind the obedience of the Old Testament believers. Give God time in secret to reveal Himself so that your soul may call the name of the place *Peniel,* which means, *"for I have seen God face to face"* (Genesis 32:30).

Complete Surrender in Prayer

My next thought is this: Let the renewal of your surrender to absolute obedience for that day be a main part of your morning prayer.

Let any confession of sin be very definite, a plucking out and cutting off of everything that has been grieving God. (See Matthew 5:29–30.) Let any prayer for grace or for a holy walk be definite also. In your prayer, ask for and accept in

The Blessings of Obedience

faith the very grace and strength you are particularly in need of. Steadfastly resolve, as you start each day, that you will keep obedience to God as your controlling principle.

There is no other possible way of entering into God's love and blessing in prayer than by getting into His will. In prayer, give yourself up completely to the blessed will of God. This will bring you more than numerous requests. Ask God to show you great mercy, enabling you to enter into His will and live there. His enabling power will make the doing of His will a blessed certainty. Let your prayer indeed be a morning sacrifice, a figurative placing of yourself as a whole burnt offering on the altar of the Lord. (See Leviticus 9:17.)

The measure of your surrender to full obedience will be the measure of your confidence toward God.

Assurance and Confidence

Then remember that true prayer and fellowship with God cannot be one-sided.

We need to be still, wait, and hear God's response. This is the Holy Spirit's duty, to be the voice of God to us. In the hidden depths of the heart, He can give a secret yet certain assurance that we are heard, that we are well-pleasing, and that the Father plans to do for us what we have asked. To receive this assurance, we need to quietly and humbly wait on God. We need to wait in the quiet faith that trusts God.

When we serve God and take His side in our prayers, He gives us the confidence that we receive what we ask. He gives us the confidence that our sacrifice of self in obedience is accepted. We can then count on the Holy Spirit to guide us into all the will of God as He plans for us to know and do it.

What glory will come to us in morning prayer, and through it into our daily lives, if we make it an hour spent with the triune God. The Father, through the Son and the Spirit, will take conscious possession of us for the day.

Consecrated Intercession

Last and best, let your prayer be intercessional on behalf of others.

In the obedience of our Lord Jesus, as in all His fellowship with the Father, the essential element was that it was all done for others. This Spirit flows through every member of the body of Christ's church. The more we know it and yield to it, the more our lives will be what God desires to make them.

The highest form of prayer is intercession. God chose Abraham, Israel, and us to make us a blessing to the world. We are *"a royal priesthood"* (1 Peter 2:9), a priestly people. As long as we only use prayer as a means of personal improvement and happiness, we cannot know its full power. Let intercession be a real longing for the souls of those around us, a real bearing of the burden of their sin and need, a real pleading for the extension of God's kingdom. Let such intercession be what our morning prayer time is consecrated to, and see what new interest and attraction it will have.

Intercession! Oh, to realize what it means! To take the name and the righteousness and the worthiness of Christ, put them on, and appear in them before God! *"In Christ's stead"* (2 Corinthians 5:20), we must pray, now that He is no longer bodily in the world, to ask God by name for the individual men and women and for the needs where His grace can do its work! In the faith of our own acceptance and of the anointing with the Spirit to prepare us for the work, we know that our prayer can *"save a soul from death"* (James 5:20) and bring the blessing of heaven upon earth.

To think that in the morning prayer hour this work can be renewed and carried on day by day!

It is in intercession, more than zeal (which works in its own strength), that true Christlikeness is cultivated. It is in intercession that a believer rises to his true nobility in the power of imparting life and blessing. We must look to intercession for any large increase of the power of God in the church and its work for men.

Morning Prayer

Maintaining His Presence

In conclusion, think again about the vital connection between obedience and morning prayer.

Without obedience, there cannot be the spiritual power to enter into the knowledge of God's Word and will. Without obedience, there cannot be the confidence, boldness, and liberty that knows the prayer is heard. Obedience is fellowship with God in His will. Without it, there is no capacity for seeing, claiming, and holding the blessing He has for us.

On the other hand, without solid, living communication with God in morning prayer, we cannot possibly maintain the life of obedience. It is there that the vow of obedience can be renewed every morning in power and be confirmed from above. It is there that the presence and fellowship can be secured that make obedience possible. In morning fellowship with Him, in the obedience of the One, we receive the strength to do all that God can ask. It is there that we receive the spiritual understanding of God's will.

God has called His children to live a wonderful, heavenly, supernatural life. Let daily, morning prayer open the gate of heaven through which its light and power stream in on your waiting heart. Walk away from your morning prayer ready to walk with God all day.

Chapter Five

Entering the Life of Full Obedience

"He...became obedient unto death."
—Philippians 2:8

After all that has been said on the life of obedience, let us consider what it is to enter this life. You might think it a mistake to take this text, in which you have obedience in its very highest perfection, as our subject in speaking of starting the obedient life. But it is no mistake. The secret of success in a race is to aim at a clearly defined goal from the start.

"He...became obedient unto death, even the death of the cross" (Philippians 2:8). There is no other Christ for any of us, no other obedience that pleases God, no other example for us to follow, no other teacher from whom to learn to obey. Christians suffer inconceivably because they do not immediately and heartily accept His obedience as the only obedience they are to aim at.

The Blessings of Obedience

To determine to be obedient unto death is a strength in the young Christian. It is at once the beauty and the glory of Christ. A share in His obedience is the highest blessing He has to give. The desire for and the surrender to it are possible to even the youngest believer.

An ancient story illustrates the kind of obedience Jesus desires from His people. A proud king, with a great army following him, demanded the submission of the king of a small but brave nation. When the ambassadors had delivered their message, the second king called one of his soldiers to stab himself. He did it at once. A second was called; he too obeyed at once. A third was summoned; and he too was obedient to death.

"Go and tell your master that I have three thousand such men; let him come." The king dared to count on men who would give up their life when the king's word called for it.

It is this type of loyal obedience that God wants. It is this obedience Christ gave. It is this obedience He teaches. We must seek to learn obedience and nothing less. From the very outset of the Christian life, let this be our aim: to avoid the fatal mistake of calling Christ "Master" yet not doing what He says.

Let all who have been convicted of the sin of disobedience, in any degree, pay close attention as we study from God's Word. He shows the way to escape from that sin and how to gain access to

Entering the Life of Full Obedience

the life Christ can give—the entrance to the life of full obedience.

Confession and Cleansing

It is easy to see that this must be the first step. In the book of Jeremiah, the prophet who spoke of the disobedience of God's people most, God said,

> *Return, thou backsliding Israel...for I am merciful....Only acknowledge thine iniquity, that...ye have not obeyed my voice, saith the* LORD. *Turn, O backsliding children...and I will bring you to Zion.* (Jeremiah 3:12–14)

At conversion, we cannot receive pardon without confession. After conversion, there cannot be deliverance from the overcoming power of sin and its disobedience without a new and deeper conviction and confession.

The thought of our disobedience must not be a vague generality. We must confess our sins, naming them specifically. We then give them up and place them in the hands of Christ. By Him, they are cleansed away. Only then can we hope to enter the way of true obedience.

Let us search our lives by the light of our Lord's teaching.

He did not come to destroy the law, but to secure its fulfillment. To the young ruler, He said,

The Blessings of Obedience

"Thou knowest the commandments" (Mark 10:19).
Let the law be our first test.

Let us take a single sin, such as that of lying.
I had a note from a young lady once, saying that
she wished to obey fully and that she felt urged to
confess an untruth she had told me. It was not a
matter of importance, yet she was right in thinking that the confession would help cast it from
her.

There is much in ordinary society that will
not stand the test of strict truthfulness. We must
be careful to obey every commandment—even
the last that forbids covetousness. Too frequently
the Christian gives way to disobedience, and he
covets and lusts after what is not his.

All this must come to a complete end. We
must confess it and, in God's strength, put it away
forever if we are to have any thought of entering
a life of full obedience.

The New Law of Love

To be merciful as the Father in heaven, to
forgive just as He does, to love enemies, to do
good to those who hate us, and to live lives of
self-sacrifice and beneficence—this is what Jesus
taught.

Let us look on an unforgiving spirit when we
are provoked or ill-used; unloving thoughts and
sharp or unkind words; and the neglect of the
call to show mercy, do good, and bless as sheer

disobedience. It must be felt, mourned over, and plucked out like a right eye before the power of full obedience can be ours. (See Matthew 5:29.)

Self is the root of all lack of love and all disobedience. Our Lord calls each of His disciples to deny himself, take up his cross, forsake everything, lose his own life, humble himself, and become the servant of all. He asks all this because self—self-will, self-pleasing, self-seeking—is simply the source of all sin.

When we give in to the flesh by overindulgence in eating and drinking; when we gratify self by seeking, accepting, or rejoicing in that which indulges our pride; when self-will is allowed to assert itself and we make provision for the fulfillment of its desire, we are guilty of disobedience to His command. This gradually clouds the soul and makes the full enjoyment of His light and peace impossible.

The Love of the Whole Heart

The Christian who has not definitely aimed to sacrifice everything, who has not determined to seek grace in order to live, is guilty of disobedience. There may be much in his religion that appears good and earnest, but he cannot possibly have the joyful consciousness of knowing he is doing the will of his Lord and keeping His commandments.

When the call is heard to come and begin a true life of obedience again, many try to slip quietly into it. They think that by more prayer and Bible study they will grow into obedience and that it will come gradually. They are greatly mistaken. The word God uses in Jeremiah might teach them their mistake: *"Turn, O backsliding children, saith the LORD"* (Jeremiah 3:14).

A soul that is in full earnest and has taken the vow of full obedience may grow out of a feeble obedience into a fuller one. But there is no growing out of disobedience into obedience. A turning back, a turning away, a decision, a crisis is needed. That only comes by very definite insight into what has been wrong and confession of the sin with shame and penitence.

Only in penance will the soul seek divine and mighty cleansing from its filthiness. Repentance prepares the consciousness for the gift of a new heart. God's Spirit will cause us to walk in His statutes.

If you hope to lead a different life, to become a man or a woman who exhibits Christlike obedience, begin by asking God for the Holy Spirit of conviction to show you all your disobedience. He will lead you, in humble confession, to the cleansing God has provided. Do not rest until you have received it.

Possibility of Obedience

The second step is to understand clearly what obedience is. To this end, we must pay careful attention to the difference between *voluntary* and *involuntary* sin. Obedience deals only with voluntary sin.

We know that the new heart that God gives His child is placed in the midst of the flesh with its sinfulness. Out of this fleshly sinfulness, even in one who is walking in true obedience, evil suggestions of pride, unlovingness, and impurities arise. They are, by nature, sinful and vile. But they are not blamed on a man as acts of transgression. They are not acts of disobedience that he can break off and cast out as he can the disobedience of which we have spoken.

The deliverance from them comes in another way, not through the will of the reborn man, by which obedience always comes, but through the cleansing power of the blood and the indwelling Spirit of Christ. As the sinful nature rises, all man can do is abhor it and trust in Christ's blood that immediately cleanses him and keeps him clean.

It is of great consequence to note the distinction. It keeps the Christian from thinking that obedience is impossible. It encourages him to seek and offer his obedience in the sphere where it can be effective. In proportion to the power of the will, the power of the Spirit can be trusted and obtained to do the cleansing work that is beyond the reach of the will.

When this difficulty has been removed, often a second one arises to make us doubt whether obedience is possible.

The Blessings of Obedience

Men connect obedience with absolute perfection. They put together all the commands of the Bible and think of all the graces these commands point to in their highest possible measure. They think of a man who displays all of the graces in full perfection as an obedient man.

How different is the demand of our Father in heaven! He takes account of each of His children's different abilities and achievements. He asks only obedience for each day—each hour—at a time. He sees whether I have, in fact, given myself up to the wholehearted performance of every known command. He sees whether I am really longing to know and do His will completely. And when His child does this in simple faith and love, the obedience is acceptable. The Spirit gives us the sweet assurance that we are well-pleasing to Him and *"then have we confidence toward God....because we keep his commandments, and do those things that are pleasing in his sight"* (1 John 3:21–22).

We can attain this degree of grace for obedience. Having faith to obtain grace for obedience is indispensable in the Christian walk. If you ask for the basis of that faith in God's Word, you can find it in God's new covenant promise, *"I will... write...[my law] in their hearts....I will put my fear in their hearts, that they shall not depart from me"* (Jeremiah 31:33; 32:40).

The problem for man with the old covenant was that it demanded, but did not provide the power for, obedience. The new covenant does. The heart means the love, the life. Having the law written on the heart means that it has taken possession of the innermost life of the renewed man. The new heart delights in God's law. The heart is willing and able to obey it.

You may doubt this because your experience does not confirm it. No wonder! A promise of God is a thing of faith. Because you do not believe it, you cannot experience it.

Do you know what invisible ink is? It is fluid that you write with but nothing shows on paper. A man who is not aware of the secret can see nothing. Tell him of the secret, and, by faith, he knows it is true. Hold the writing up to the sun or put some chemical on it, and out comes the secret writing. God's law is written in your heart. If you believe this firmly and say to God that His law is there in your innermost part, you can hold up that heart to the light and heat of the Holy Spirit, and you will find that His law is there. When the law is written on your heart, you will have the fervent love of God's commands, with the power to obey them. How plain, how certain, how all-sufficient the provision is that has been made in the new covenant, the covenant of grace, for securing our obedience!

Napoleon's doctor was trying to extract a bullet lodged in the heart region of one of his soldiers, when the soldier cried, "Cut deeper, you will find *Napoleon* carved there."

The Blessings of Obedience

Christian, believe that God's law lives in your innermost being. Speak in faith the words of David and of Christ: *"I delight to do thy will, O my God; yea, thy law is within* [written on] *my heart"* (Psalm 40:8).

Faith in this psalm will assure you that obedience is possible. Such faith will help you in the life of true obedience.

Obedience by Surrender

"Return [to me], *ye backsliding children, and I will heal your backslidings"* (Jeremiah 3:22), God said to Israel. They were His people but had turned from Him. Their return had to be immediate and entire. To turn our backs on the divided life of disobedience and say, in the faith of God's grace, "I will obey," may only last for a moment.

The power for obedience, to take the vow and keep it, comes from the loving Christ. I have said before that the power of obedience lies in the mighty influence of Jesus Christ's living, personal presence. As long as we take our knowledge of God's will from a book or from men, we can only fail. If we think of Jesus as our Lord and strength, we can obey Him.

The voice that commands us is the voice that inspires. The eye that guides us is the eye that encourages. Christ becomes everything to us—the Master who commands, the Example who teaches, the Helper who strengthens. Turn from

Entering the Life of Full Obedience

your life of disobedience to Christ. Give yourself up to Him in faith.

Let Him have everything. Give up your life to be as full of Him, His presence, His will, and His service as He can make it. Give yourself to Him so that He may have you wholly for Himself as a vessel, a channel, that He can fill with Himself, with His life and love for men, in His blessed service.

When a soul sees this new thing in Christ, the power for continual obedience, it needs a new faith to take in the special blessing of His great redemption. The faith that only understood His "[becoming] *obedient unto death*" as a motive to love and obedience now learns to take the word as Scripture speaks it: *"Let this mind be in you, which was also in Christ Jesus, who...humbled himself, and became obedient unto death"* (Philippians 2:5–6, 8). It believes that Christ put His own mind and Spirit into us, and in the faith of this, His Spirit prepares us to live and act in obedience.

God sent Christ into the world to restore obedience to its place in our hearts and lives. His purpose is to restore man to his place in the obedience to God. Christ came and, becoming obedient unto death, proved what the only true obedience is. He brought it about and perfected it in Himself as a life that He won through death. He now communicates this obedience to us. The Christ who loves us, lives in us, leads, teaches, and strengthens us, is the Christ who was obedient unto death. *"Obedient unto death"* is the essence of the life He gives. Will we not accept it and trust Him to create it in us?

Would you like to enter into the blessed life of obedience? See, here is the open gate. Christ says, *"I am the door"* (John 10:7). Christ says, *"I am the way"* (John 14:6). He is the *"new and living way"* (Hebrews 10:20).

We begin to see it. Our disobedience comes from our not knowing Christ correctly. Obedience is only possible in a life of unceasing fellowship with Him. The inspiration of His voice, the light of His eyes, the grasp of His hand make it possible, make it certain.

Come, let us bow down and yield ourselves to this Christ, obedient to death in the faith that He makes us partakers, with Himself, of all He is and has.

Chapter Six

The Obedience of Faith

"By faith Abraham, when he was called to go out into a place which he should after receive for an inheritance, obeyed; and he went out, not knowing whither he went."
—Hebrews 11:8

Abraham believed there was a land of Canaan of which God had spoken. He believed it was a *"land of promise"* (Hebrews 11:9), secured to him as an inheritance. He believed that God would bring him there, show it to him, and give it to him. In that faith, he dared go out, *"not knowing whither he went."* In the blessed ignorance of faith, he trusted God, obeyed Him, and received the inheritance.

The land of promise that is set before us is the blessed life of obedience. We have heard God's call to go out and dwell there; about this there can be no mistake. We have heard the promise of Christ to bring us there and to give us possession of the land. This, too, is clear and sure.

We have surrendered ourselves to our Lord and asked our Father to make all this true in us. Our desire now is that all our life and work will be lifted up to the level of a holy and joyful obedience, and that through us God may make obedience the keynote of the Christian life we aim at promoting in others. Our aim is high. We can only reach it by a new inflow of the power that comes from above. Only by a faith that springs from new vision and clasps the power of heaven, as secured by Jesus Christ, can we obey and obtain the promise.

As we think of all this, of cultivating in ourselves and others the conviction that we live only to please Him, some are ready to say, "This is not a land of promise we are called to enter, but a life of burden, difficulty, and certain failure."

Do not say this, my friend! God calls you to a land of promise. Come and prove what He can work in you. Come and experience the nobility of a Christlike obedience that is unto death. Come and see what a blessing God will give the person who, with Christ, gives himself completely to the holy will of God. Trust in the glory of this good land of wholehearted obedience, in God who calls you to it, in Christ who will bring you into it, and in the Holy Spirit who dwells and works there. He who believes will enter.

The Obedience of Faith

Five simple phrases express the disposition of a believing heart that enters that life in the good land: I see it, desire it, expect it, accept it, and trust Christ for it.

Faithful Vision

I have been trying to show you the map of the land and to indicate the most important places in the land, the points where God meets and blesses the soul. What we need now is to settle the question quietly and definitely in faith. Is there really such a land of promise where continuous obedience is completely possible?

As long as there is any doubt on this point, it is out of the question to go up and possess the land. Think of Abraham's faith. It rested in God's omnipotence and His faithfulness. I have put before you the promises of God. Look at another of them: *"A new heart also will I give you....And I will put my spirit within you, and cause you to walk in my statutes, and ye shall keep my judgments, and do them"* (Ezekiel 36:26–27). Here is God's covenant promise. He adds, *"I the LORD have spoken it, and I will do it"* (v. 36). He endeavors to cause and enable you to obey. In Christ and the Holy Spirit, He has made the most wonderful provision for fulfilling His promise.

Do what Abraham did. Fix your heart on God. *"He staggered not at the promise of God through unbelief; but was strong in faith, giving glory to God; and being fully persuaded that, what he had promised, he was able also to perform"* (Romans 4:20–21). God's omnipotence was Abraham's pillar. Let it be yours.

God gives us many promises in the Bible, promises that require His power in order to come to pass. He promises us a blameless heart and a life that keeps His commandments. His working in us, and our trust that He is working in us, will make this life of full obedience possible. Let the assurance that a life of full obedience is possible permeate your thoughts. Faith can see the invisible and the impossible. Gaze on the vision until your heart says, "It must be true. It is true. There is a life promised that I have never yet known."

Faith's Desire

When I read the gospel story and see how ready the sick, the blind, and the needy were to believe Christ's word, I often ask myself what it was that made them so much more ready to believe than we are. The answer I find in the Word is this: The one great difference lies in the honesty and intensity of the desire. They desired deliverance with their whole hearts. Jesus did not need to plead with them to make them willing to take His blessing.

It should be the same with us. Everyone wishes, in some way, to be better than they are. But how few people truly *"hunger and thirst after righteousness"* (Matthew 5:6). How few people intensely long and cry after a life of close obedience and the continual consciousness of being pleasing to God.

There can be no strong faith without strong desire. Desire is the great motivating power in the universe. It was God's desire to save us that moved Him to send His Son. It is desire that moves men to study and work and suffer. It is only the desire for salvation that brings a sinner to Christ. It is the desire for God and the closest possible fellowship with Him—the desire to be exactly what He would have us be and to have as much of His will as possible—that will make the promised land attractive to us. It is this desire that will inspire us to forsake everything to get our full share in the obedience of Christ.

And how can the desire be awakened? Shame on us that we need to ask the question, that the most desirable of all things—likeness to God in union with His will—has so little attraction for us! Let us take it as a sign of our blindness and beg God to give us, by His Spirit, enlightened eyes of the heart. Then we may know *"the riches of the glory of his inheritance"* (Ephesians 1:18), waiting upon the life of true obedience. Let us turn and gaze, in this light of God's Spirit, on the obedient life as a thing that is possible, certain, divinely secured, and divinely blessed. Let us look until our faith begins to burn with desire and we say, "I long to have it. With my whole heart I will seek it."

The Blessings of Obedience

Expectant Faith

The difference between desire and expectation is great. It is a great step forward when desire grows into expectation, and the soul begins to say, "I am sure spiritual blessing is for me, and, though I do not see how, I confidently expect to obtain it."

The life of obedience is no longer an unattainable ideal held out by God to make us strive to at least get a little nearer to it. It is now a reality meant for flesh and blood here on earth. Expect it. It is meant for you. Expect God to make it true.

Many things may hinder this expectation. Your past failures, disagreeable temperament, unfavorable circumstances, feeble faith, your difficulty as to what such a devotion—obedience to the point of death—may demand, and a conscious lack of power for it can make you say, "It may be for others, but it is not for me."

Do not speak this way. You are leaving God out of the picture. Expect your blessing! Look up to His power and His love, and say, "It is for me!"

From his youth, Gerhard Tersteegen sought to serve the Lord. After a time, he lost the sense of God's grace. For five long years, he was far away on the great sea of spiritual isolation, where neither sun nor stars appear. "But," he said, "my hope was in Jesus."

The Obedience of Faith

All at once a light broke on him that never went out. He wrote his famous letter to the Lord Jesus. "From this evening to all eternity, Thy will, not mine be done. Command and rule and reign in me. I yield up myself without reserve, and I promise, with Thy help and power, rather to give up the last drop of my blood than knowingly or willingly be untrue or disobedient to Thee."

This was his obedience to the point of death.

Set your heart on it and expect it. The same God still lives. Set your hope on Him, and He will do it.

Accepting in Faith

To accept is more than to expect. Many wait and hope yet never possess because they do not accept.

To all who have not accepted and feel as if they are not ready to accept—start by expecting. If the expectation is from the heart and is truly set on God Himself, it will lead the soul to accept. To those who say they do expect, it is time for the next step—accept. Faith has that wonderful, God-given power of saying, "I accept, I take, I have."

It is the lack of definite faith—faith that claims and takes hold of the spiritual blessing we desire—that makes so many prayers appear fruitless. Not every believer is ready for such an act of faith. Another reason a believer's prayers appear to be fruitless is that the believer simply does not have the capacity to accept a blessing. Often there is no true conviction of the sin of disobedience or any sorrow for the lack of conviction.

In addition, believers may not have a strong longing or resolution to obey God in everything.

Many do not even have the necessary deep interest in the Scripture message that shows how God wants to perfect us. In short, the Christian is content to remain a baby. He only wants to drink the milk of consolation. He is not able to tolerate the strong meat that Jesus ate—doing the will of His Father.

Despite our human frailty, God asks us to accept the grace for this wondrous new life of obedience. Accept it now. Without this, your act of consecration will amount to little. Without this, your goal of trying to be more obedient will fail. Has God not shown you that there is an entirely new position for you to take, a position of simple, childlike obedience? His grace makes it possible for you to daily obey every command He gives you through the Holy Spirit. Christians can live in simple, childlike dependence on God's grace for obedience.

I beg you, even now, to take that position, to make that surrender, to take that grace. Accept and enter the true life of faith and the unceasing obedience of faith. May your faith be as unlimited

The Obedience of Faith

and solid as God's promise and power. Your simple, childlike obedience will be as unlimited as your faith. Ask God for His aid, and accept everything that He has offered you.

Trusting Jesus Christ for Everything

"For all the promises of God in him are yea, and in him Amen, unto the glory of God by us" (2 Corinthians 1:20). It is possible that as I have spoken of the life of obedience there have been questions and difficulties arising for which you cannot find answers.

You may feel as if you cannot take it in all at once or reconcile it with all of your old habits of thought and speech and action. You fear you will not be able to bring everything immediately into subjection to this supreme principle. Do everything as the will of God. Do everything as obedience to Him.

There is one answer, one deliverance from all these fears. It is Jesus Christ. He is the living Savior, who knows all. He asks you to trust yourself to Him for the wisdom and the power to always walk in the obedience of faith.

We have seen, more than once, how His whole redemption, as He made it come to be, is nothing but obedience. As He communicates redemption, the message is still the same. He gives us the spirit of obedience as the spirit of life. This spirit comes to us each moment through Him.

The Blessings of Obedience

Jesus Himself keeps charge of our obedience. He offers Himself to us as our surety for its maintenance and asks us to trust Him for it. It is in Jesus Himself that all our fears are removed, all our needs supplied, all our desires met. *"Delight thyself also in the LORD; and he shall give thee the desires of thine heart"* (Psalm 37:4). Just as He, the Righteous One, is your righteousness, He, the Obedient One, is also your obedience.

Will you not trust Him for it? What faith sees, desires, expects, and accepts, surely it can trust Christ to give and work.

Will you not take the opportunity today of giving glory to God and His Son by trusting Jesus now to lead you into the Promised Land? Look up to your glorified Lord in heaven. In His strength, renew your vow of allegiance, your vow to never willingly do anything that would offend Him.

Trust Him for the faith to make the vow, the heart to keep it, and the strength to carry it out. Trust Him—dare to join in an act of communion—and be assured that He promises and devotes Himself to honor your act. He does this to bring honor to God through us.

Chapter Seven

More about Obedience

*"Gather up the fragments that remain,
that nothing be lost."*
—John 6:12

In this chapter, I wish to mention some points not yet touched on or expressed with sufficient clarity. I hope that they will help someone who truly desires to grow in obedience to Jesus Christ.

First, let me warn against a misunderstanding of the expression "learning obedience."

We are likely to think that absolute obedience—obedience unto death—is something we can only learn gradually. This is a great mistake with harmful potential. What we have to learn, and do learn gradually, is to practice new and more difficult commands. But as to the principle, Christ wants us to make the vow of entire obedience from the very beginning of our Christian walk.

A little child of five can be as implicitly obedient as a youth of eighteen. The difference between the two lies not in the principle but in the nature of the work demanded.

Though Christ's obedience to the point of death came literally at the end of His life, the spirit of His obedience was the same from the beginning. Wholehearted obedience is not the end but the beginning of our learning in Christ. The goal is qualification for God's service when obedience has placed us fully at God's disposal. A heart yielded to God in unreserved obedience is the one condition of growth in the spiritual knowledge of God's will.

Young Christian, get this matter settled at once. Remember God's rule—all for all. Give Him all, and He will give you all. Consecration avails nothing unless it means presenting yourself as a living sacrifice to do nothing but the will of God. The vow of entire obedience is the seed that must be planted by anyone who wants to grow in obedience and be closer to Christ.

Learning to Know God's Will

This unreserved surrender to obey is the first condition of entering Christ's school of obedience.

More about Obedience

It is the only frame of mind for receiving instruction on God's will for us.

God has a general will for all of His children. We can learn it, in some measure, from the Bible. But there is also a special, individual application of these commands—God's will concerning us personally—that only the Holy Spirit can teach. He will only teach God's will to those who have taken the vow of obedience.

This is why there are so many unanswered prayers for God to make known His will. Jesus said, *"If any man will do his will, he shall know of the doctrine, whether it be of God"* (John 7:17). If a man's will is determined to do God's will, and he does it to the extent that he knows it, he will know more about what God has to teach him.

It is simply what is true of every scholar with the art he studies, of every apprentice with his trade, of every man in business—doing is the one condition of truly knowing. Likewise, our capacity for receiving the true knowledge of God's will for us rests in our vowing to do, then our obeying ,God's will, as far as we know it and as He reveals it to us. In connection with this, let me focus on three things.

First, seek to have a deep sense of your great ignorance of God's will and your inability through your own effort to know it correctly. Being conscious of your ignorance will make you teachable. *"The meek will he guide...in his way"* (Psalm 25:9). Those who humbly confess their need of teaching are meek and humble. Head knowledge only gives human thoughts without power. God, by His Spirit, gives a living knowledge that enters the love of the heart and works effectively.

Second, cultivate a strong faith that God will make you know wisdom in the hidden part— your heart. (See Psalm 51:6.) This thought may appear strange. Learn that God's working, the place where He gives His life and light, is in the heart. He works at a deeper level than all our thoughts.

Any uncertainty about God's will makes a joyful obedience impossible. Believe confidently that the Father is willing to make known what He wants you to do. Count on Him for this. Expect it with certainty.

Third, remembering the dark and deceitful nature of the flesh and carnal mind, ask God earnestly for the searching and convincing light of the Holy Spirit. There may be many things that you have been accustomed to think are lawful or allowable that your Father wants to change.

Assuming that these things are the will of God because you and others think so may effectively shut you out from knowing God's will in other things. Bring everything, without reserve, to the judgment of the Word as explained and applied by the Holy Spirit. Serve God and wait for Him to lead you to know that everything you are and do is pleasing in His sight.

More about Obedience

Obedience Even to Death

A deeper aspect of complete obedience even to death does not usually come up in the early stages of the Christian life. Yet every believer should be aware of the privilege that awaits him. Wholehearted obedience can bring the believer into an experience where obedience to God will lead to his death.

Let us see what this means. During our Lord's life, His resistance to sin and the world was perfect and complete. Yet His final deliverance from their temptations and His victory over their power—achieved by His obedience—was not complete until He had died to the earthly life and to sin. In that death, He gave up His life, in perfect helplessness, to the Father's hands, waiting for the Father to raise Him up. It was through death that He received the fullness of His new life and glory. Only through death, by giving up His life, could obedience lead Him into the glory of God.

The believer shares with Christ in this death to sin. In regeneration, he is baptized by the Holy Spirit into obedience. Due to ignorance and unbelief, he may know little by experience of this entire death to sin. When the Holy Spirit reveals to the believer what he possesses in Christ, and the believer takes hold of it in faith, the Spirit works in him the very same disposition that animated Christ in His death.

Christ completely surrendered control of His life to God. He offered a helpless committal of His

The Blessings of Obedience

Spirit into the Father's hands. This was the complete fulfillment of the Father's command. Out of the perfect self-oblivion of the grave, He entered the glory of the Father.

It is into this fellowship that a believer is brought. He finds, even in the most unreserved obedience for which God's Spirit prepares him, there is still a secret element of self and self-will. He longs to be delivered from it. He is taught in God's Word that this can only be through death.

The Spirit helps him to claim more fully that he is indeed dead to sin in Christ. The Spirit also shows him that the power of this death can work mightily in him. He is made willing to be obedient unto death. This entire death to self makes him truly nothing. In this he gains full entrance into the life of Christ.

To see the need of this entire death to self, to be made willing to do it, to be led into the entire self-emptying and humility of our Lord Jesus—this is the highest lesson our obedience has to learn. This is, indeed, the Christlike obedience, even to death. In due time, God Himself will teach more on this particular subject to those who are entirely faithful.

The Voice of Conscience

In regard to the knowledge of God's will, we must give conscience its place and submit to its authority.

More about Obedience

There are a thousand little things in which the law of nature or education teaches us what is right and good. But even earnest Christians do not hold themselves bound to obey these things. Remember Jesus said, *"He that is faithful in that which is least is faithful also in much"* (Luke 16:10). If you are unfaithful with small things, who will trust you with larger things? Not God.

If the voice of conscience tells you that one course of action is nobler or better, and you choose another because it is easier or pleasing to self, you block yourself from the teaching of the Spirit by disobeying the voice of God in nature. A strong desire to always do the right thing is a desire to do God's will. Paul wrote, *"I lie not, my conscience also bearing me witness in the Holy Ghost"* (Romans 9:1). The Holy Spirit speaks through conscience. If you disobey and hurt your conscience, you make it impossible for God to speak to you.

One who obeys God's will also respects the voice of his conscience. This holds true with regard to eating and drinking, sleeping and resting, spending money and seeking pleasure. Everything should be brought into subjection to the will of God.

If you desire to live the life of true obedience, make sure you maintain a good conscience before God and never knowingly indulge in anything that is contrary to His mind. George Müller attributed all of his happiness, during seventy years, to obedience and his love of God's Word. He maintained a good conscience in everything, not continuing in any action he knew was contrary to God's will. Conscience is the guardian God gives to warn you when you are doing wrong.

According to the light you have, listen to your conscience. Ask God, by the teaching of His will, to give it more light. Seek the witness of conscience that you are acting according to that light.

Your conscience will become your encouragement and your helper. It will give you the confidence, both that your obedience is accepted and that your prayer for increasing knowledge of God's will is heard.

Legal and Evangelical Obedience

Even when a Christian has taken the vow of unreserved obedience, there may still be two sorts of obedience. One is the obedience of the law, and the other is that of the Gospel. Just as there are two testaments (an old and a new), there are also two styles of religion, two ways of serving God. This is what Paul spoke about in Romans when he said, *"Sin shall not have dominion over you: for ye are not under the law, but under grace"* (Romans 6:14). He spoke more about our being *"free from that law"* (Romans 7:3), *"that we should serve in newness of spirit, and not in the oldness of the letter"* (v. 6). Again he reminded us, *"For ye have not received the spirit of bondage again to fear; but ye have received the Spirit of adoption"* (Romans 8:15).

These verses clearly point to the danger of a Christian acting as if he was under the law—serving in the oldness of the letter and in the spirit of bondage. One great cause of the feebleness of so much Christian living is that it is under law more than under grace. Let us see what the difference is.

What the law demands from us, grace promises and performs for us. The law deals with what we should do, whether we can do it or not. The law, motivating us out of fear and love, stirs us up to do our best. But it gives no real strength and thus only leads to failure and condemnation. Grace points to what we cannot do and offers to do it for us and in us.

The law comes with commands on stone or in a book. Grace comes in a living, gracious Person who gives His presence and His power.

The law promises life if we obey. Grace gives life, even the Holy Spirit, with the assurance that we can obey.

Human nature is always prone to slip back out of grace into law and secretly trust in its own ability to do its best. The promises of grace are so divine, the gift of the Holy Spirit to complete everything in us is so wonderful, that few believe it. This is why they never dare to take the vow of obedience. Or, having taken it, they turn away again.

I beg you, study well what gospel obedience is. The Gospel is good news. Its obedience is part of the good news—that grace, by the Holy Spirit, will do everything in you. Believe, and let every undertaking to obey God be in the joyous hope that comes from faith in Christ's abundance of grace, in the mighty indwelling of the Holy Spirit, in the blessed love of Jesus, whose abiding presence makes obedience possible and certain.

The Obedience of Love

Obedience arising out of love is one of the special and most beautiful aspects of gospel obedience. The grace that promises to complete everything through the Holy Spirit is the gift of eternal love. The Lord Jesus (who takes charge of our obedience, teaches it, and, by His presence, secures it to us) is He who loved us to the death, who loves us with a love that surpasses our understanding.

Nothing can receive or know love but a loving heart. It is this loving heart that enables us to obey. Obedience is the loving response to the divine love resting on us. It is the only access to a fuller enjoyment of that love.

How our Lord insisted on this in His farewell discourse! He repeated it three times in John 14: *"If ye love me, keep my commandments....He that hath my commandments, and keepeth them, he it* re about Obedience

n me....If a man love me, he will keep
(John 14:15, 21, 23).

)t clear that love alone can give the obe-
;us asks, and that love alone can receive
ing Jesus gives to obedience? Loving obe-
;ives the believer a cycle of blessings. The
to obey the Lord and accept Jesus brings
gift of the Holy Spirit living within us,
s to the Father's love, and Christ's own love.
;e three, in turn, assure success in the obedi-
c.. life.

In the next chapter of John's gospel, he looked at another side of obedience and showed how it leads to the enjoyment of God's love. Jesus kept His Father's commandments and now lives in His love. If we keep His commandments, we will also live in His love. Jesus proved His love by giving His life for us. We are His friends, and we will enjoy His love if we do what He commands us. Obedience is the one indispensable link between His loving us first and our love in response, as well as between our love and His fuller love in response to ours. True, full obedience is impossible unless we live and love. *"For this is the love of God, that we keep his commandments: and his commandments are not grievous"* (1 John 5:3).

Beware of falling into the legal obedience trap, which is struggling to live a life of true obedience out of a sense of duty. Ask God to show you the *"newness of life"* (Romans 6:4) that will bring you the life of vibrant obedience, one full

The Blessings of Obedience

of blessings. Claim the promise, "[I] *will circumcise thine heart...to love the LORD thy God with all thine heart, and....thou shalt return and obey the voice of the LORD* (Deuteronomy 30:6, 8).

Believe in the love of God and the grace of our Lord Jesus. Believe that the Holy Spirit whom Jesus gave you enables you to love and walk in God's statutes. Only the continual, loving presence of Jesus can keep you in continual obedience.

Is Obedience Possible?

The question of the possibility of obedience lies at the very root of life. The secret, half-unconscious thought that always living a pleasing life before God is beyond our reach eats away the very root of our strength. I urge you to give a definite answer to this question.

If, in the light of God's provision for obedience—His promise of working all His good pleasure in you, His giving you a new heart, the indwelling of His Son and Spirit—you still believe obedience is not possible, ask God to open your eyes to truly know His will. If you agree to the truth theoretically, yet fear to give yourself up to this life, ask God to open your eyes. Ask Him to let you know His will for you. Beware, lest the secret fear of having to give up too much, having to become too odd and entirely devoted to God, keeps you back. Beware of seeking just enough

More about Obedience

religion to ease your conscience, then not desiring to do and be and give God everything He is worthy of. Beware, above all, of limiting God, of making Him a liar by refusing to believe what He has said He can and will do for you.

If our learning obedience is to bring us any blessing, we must not rest until we have written this down: "Daily obedience, doing everything God desires, is possible for me. With His strength, I yield myself to Him, trusting Him to accomplish my obedience."

Remember this one condition. It is not the strength of your own resolve or effort, but the unceasing presence of Christ and the continuous teaching, grace, and power of the Holy Spirit, that brings the blessing of obedience. Christ the Obedient One, living in you, will secure your obedience. Obedience will be to you a life of love and joy in His fellowship.

Chapter Eight

Obeying His Final Command

"Go ye therefore, and teach all nations."
—Matthew 28:19

*"Go ye into all the world, and preach the gospel
to every creature."*
—Mark 16:15

*"As thou hast sent me into the world, even so have
I also sent them into the world."*
—John 17:18

*"But ye shall receive power, after that the Holy
Ghost is come upon you: and ye shall be witnesses
unto...the uttermost part of the earth."*
—Acts 1:8

All these words speak of nothing less than the spirit of world conversion: *"all nations," "all the world," "every creature," "the uttermost part of the earth."* Each expression indicates that the heart of Christ was set on claiming His rightful dominion over the world He had redeemed and won for Himself. He counted on His disciples to carry out this work. As He stood at the foot of the throne, ready to ascend and reign, He told them, *"All power is given unto me in heaven and in earth"* (Matthew 28:18). He immediately pointed them to *"the utermost part of the earth"* as the object of His and their desire and efforts. As the King on the throne, He Himself would be their Helper. *"Lo, I am with you alway"* (Matthew 28:20).

Christians are to be the advance guard of His conquering hosts, even to the far corners of the world. Jesus Himself will carry on the war. He seeks to inspire His people with His own assurance of victory. It is His own purpose to make winning the world back to God the only thing worth living or dying for.

Christ does not teach or argue, ask or plead. He simply commands. He had trained His disciples to obedience. He had attached them to Himself in a love that can obey. He had already breathed His own resurrection Spirit into them. He could count on them. He dared to say to them, *"Go ye into all the world."*

Formerly, during His life on earth, they had more than once expressed their doubts about the possibility of fulfilling His commands. But here, as quietly and simply as He spoke these divine words, His disciples accepted them. No sooner

Obeying His Final Command

had He ascended than they went to the appointed place to wait for the heavenly power from their Lord in heaven. This heavenly power would equip them for the heavenly work of making all the nations His disciples. They accepted the command and passed it on to those who, through them, believed on His name.

Within a generation, simple men, whose names we do not even know, had preached the Gospel in Antioch, Rome, and the regions beyond. The command was passed on and taken up into the heart and life, as meant for all ages, as meant for every disciple.

The command is for each of us, too. In the church, there is no single, privileged clan to which the honor belongs or any servile clan on which the duty of carrying the Gospel to every creature rests. The life Christ imparts is His own life; the Spirit He breathes is His very own Spirit; the one disposition He works is His own self-sacrificing love. It lies in the very nature of His salvation that every member of His body, in full and healthy access with Him, feels urged to give what he has received.

The command is no arbitrary law from the outside. By consenting to and obeying His final command, we acknowledge that we live to glorify the Father. As part of His church body, we are His representatives on earth. We confirm that His love and His will now carry us through the work of winning lost souls back to Christ.

The Blessings of Obedience

How terribly the church has failed in obeying the command! How many Christians there are who never knew there was such a command! Many hear of it but do not earnestly desire to obey it. Many seek to obey it, but only in a way that is convenient.

We have been studying what obedience is. We have said that we give ourselves up to wholehearted obedience. Surely we are prepared to gladly listen to anything that can help us understand and carry out our Lord's last and greatest command to give the Gospel to every creature.

Let me tell you what I have to say by giving you three simple points—accept His command, place yourself entirely at His disposal, and begin immediately to live for His kingdom.

Accepting His Command

There are several things that weaken the force of this command. We have the impression that a command given to everyone and so general in its nature is not as binding as one that is personal and specific. We tend to believe that if others do not do their part, our share of the blame is comparatively small. We feel that where the difficulties are extreme, obedience cannot be an absolute demand. Finally, we think if we are willing to do our best, this is all anyone can ask of us.

Brothers and sisters, this is not obedience! This is not the spirit in which the first disciples accepted the Great Commission. This is not the spirit in which we wish to live with our beloved Lord. We need to say, each one of us, "Even if there is no one else, by His grace, I will give myself and my life to live for His kingdom. Let me, for a moment, separate myself from all others and think of my personal relationship to Jesus."

I am a member of Christ's body. He expects every member to be at His disposal, to be animated by His Spirit, to live for what He is and does. It is the same with my body. I carry every healthy member with me day by day in the assurance that I can count on it to do its part. Our Lord has taken me so completely up into His body that He can ask and expect nothing else from me. I have so completely yielded myself to Him that there is no thought of my wanting anything except to know and do His will.

Let me use the illustration of the vine and the branches. The branch has the same single purpose for its existence as the vine—bearing fruit. If I really am a branch of Christ's vine, my purpose, as much as His, is to bring forth fruit—to live and work for the salvation of men. Look at another illustration. Christ bought me with His blood. No slave conquered by force or purchased by money was ever so entirely the property of his master as my soul, which is redeemed and won by Christ's blood. My soul is given up and bound to Him by love. My soul is His property, for Him alone to do with it what He pleases. He claims my soul by divine right, working through the Holy Spirit in an infinite power, and I have given my full consent to live only for His kingdom and service. This is my joy and my glory.

There was a time when it was different. To illustrate this, notice that there are two ways in which a man can bestow his money or service on another. There was once a slave, who by his trade earned large sums of money. All the money went to the master. The master was kind and treated the slave well. Finally, by saving the money his master had allowed him, the slave was able to purchase his liberty. In time, the master became impoverished and had to come to his former slave for help. The slave was not only able but willing to give it. He gave liberally, in gratitude for the master's former kindness.

You can immediately see the difference between the giving of his money and service when he was a slave and when he was free. In the former case, he gave everything because he and his earnings belonged to the master. In the latter, he gave only what he chose.

In which way should we give to Christ Jesus? I am afraid many give as if they are free to give what they choose. They give what they think they can afford. The believer, who is now purchased by Christ's blood, delights in knowing that he is the bondservant of redeeming love. He lays everything he has at his Master's feet.

Obeying His Final Command

Have you ever wondered why the disciples accepted the great command so easily and so heartily? They came fresh from Calvary, where they had seen Christ's blood. They had met the Risen One, and He had breathed His Spirit into them. During the forty days, *"he through the Holy Ghost had given commandments unto the apostles"* (Acts 1:2). Jesus was their Savior, Master, Friend, and Lord. His Word was divine power. They could do nothing but obey. Oh, let us bow at His feet and yield to the Holy Spirit. Let Him reveal and assert His mighty claim, and without hesitation let us wholeheartedly accept this command as our one life purpose. Give the Gospel to every creature!

Place Yourself at His Disposal

The last great command has been so prominently urged in connection with foreign missions that many are inclined to confine it to that. This is a serious mistake. Our Lord's words, *"Teach all nations...to observe all things whatsoever I have commanded you"* (Matthew 28:19–20), tell us what our aim is to be. Our aim is nothing less than to make every man a true disciple, living in holy obedience to all Christ's will.

What a work there is to be done in our churches and so-called Christian communities before we can say that the command has been carried out! And what a need for every believer in the church to realize that this work is the only purpose of its existence! The complete Gospel brought to every creature—this is the mission. This should be the passion of every redeemed soul. For this alone is the Spirit, likeness, and life of Christ formed in you.

If there is one thing the church needs to preach in the power of the Holy Spirit, it is the absolute and immediate duty of every child of God not only to take part in this work, but also to give himself to Christ the Master to be guided and used. Therefore, I say to every reader who has taken the vow of full obedience, Can we dare to consider ourselves true Christians if we have not done so? Immediately place yourself at Christ's disposal.

This last command, to take the Gospel to every creature, is as binding as God's first great command, *"Thou shalt love the Lord thy God with all thy heart"* (Luke 10:27). Before you know what your work may be, and before you feel any special desire, call, or ability for a particular work, if you are willing to accept the command, place yourself at His disposal.

It is His promise as Master to train, guide, and use you. Do not be afraid. Come out of the selfish religion that puts your own will and comfort first. Come out of the religion that lets you give Christ only what you deem necessary. Let the Master know He can have you completely. Enroll yourself with Him now as a volunteer for His service.

Obeying His Final Command

Obey Christ's call, even if it is to give yourself to foreign missionary work. These simple words, "It is my desire, if it is God's will, to become a foreign missionary," have brought countless blessings into thousands of lives! Meanwhile, some who cannot travel abroad have missed countless blessings because they did not simply resolve, "By the grace of God, I devote my life completely to the service of Christ's kingdom."

The foreign volunteer may struggle less with this resolution because he has broken the ties to those things that could hinder him. The devoted Christian who stays at home may not need this separation from home. Yet he needs all the help that a pledge to loyalty, given in secret or in union with others, can bring. The Holy Spirit can use this commitment to lead lives to be entirely devoted to God.

Accept the Great Commission with your whole heart. Place yourselves entirely at His disposal.

Acting on Your Vow of Obedience

Whatever your circumstances, it is your privilege to have within reach souls that can be won for God. All around you, there are countless Christian ministries that invite your help and offer you theirs. Look on yourself as bought by Christ for His service and as blessed with His Spirit to give you His disposition. Take up humbly, but boldly, your life calling to participate in the great work

The Blessings of Obedience

of winning the world back to God. Whether you are led by God to join one of the many agencies already at work or to walk in a more solitary path, remember not to view the work as your church's, society's, or as your own, but as the Lord's.

Always remember Paul's instructions, *"What-soever ye do, do it heartily, as to the Lord"* (Colossians 3:23). You are a servant who is under orders and simply carrying them out. Then your work will not come between you and your fellowship with Christ, but it will link you inseparably to Him, His strength, and His approval.

It is easy to become so engrossed in the human part of our work that we lose sight of its spiritual character and the need for God's supernatural power. When Jesus is our focus, His work fills us with heavenly joy and hope. Keep your eyes on your Master, on your King, on His throne.

Before He gave the command and pointed His servants to the great field of the world, He first drew their eyes to Himself on the throne. *"All power is given unto me in heaven and in earth"* (Matthew 28:18). It is the vision, the faith of Christ on the throne, that assures us of His sufficient, divine power. Do not obey as you would a command, but think of yourself as obeying the living, almighty Lord of glory. Faith in Him will give you heavenly strength.

These words followed: *"Lo, I am with you alway"* (v. 20). We not only need Christ on the

Obeying His Final Command

throne, but we also need His abiding presence, working for us and through us. Christ's power in heaven, Christ's presence on earth—between these two pillar promises lies the gate through which the church enters the conquest of the world. Each of us must follow Jesus, receive from Him our orders as to our share in the work, and never falter in our vow of obedience that has given itself to live only for His will and work.

Such a beginning will be a training time, preparing us fully to know and follow His leading. If His pleading call for the millions of dying heathens comes to us, we will be ready to go. If His providence does not permit our going, our devotion at home will be as complete and intense as if we had gone. Whether it is at home or abroad, if the ranks of the obedient are filled up, Christ will have His heart's desire. The Gospel will find its way to every creature.

Blessed Son of God! Here I am. By Your grace, I give my life to the carrying out of Your last great command. Let my heart be as Your heart. Let my weakness be as Your strength. In Your name, I take the vow of entire and everlasting obedience. Amen.

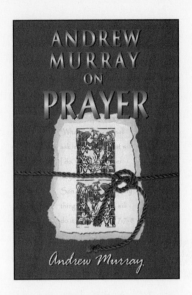

Andrew Murray on Prayer
Andrew Murray

Combining seven of Andrew Murray's most treasured works on prayer, this book will give you biblical guidelines for effective communication with God. Discover essential keys to developing a vital prayer life, including how to receive clear direction from the Lord, see your unsaved loved ones come to Christ, and overcome temptation. Lovingly explained, the principles presented here will permanently transform your prayer life!

ISBN: 0-88368-528-0 • Trade • 656 pages

WHITAKER HOUSE

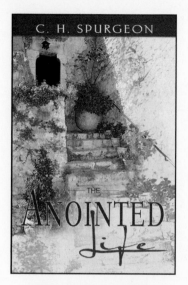

The Anointed Life
Charles H. Spurgeon

With a compassionate heart, Charles Spurgeon addresses
your doubts, fears, and questions about salvation, faith,
and how to live a life that pleases God. In a compelling
blend of down-to-earth common sense and heavenly
wisdom, he explains the great truths of forgiveness,
redemption, and power for living *The Anointed Life* in Christ.
Once you understand these truths, you can move forward
with confidence and serve God with true joy. Come—
renew your faith, enrich your spirit, and empower your life.

ISBN: 0-88368-473-X • Trade • 624 pages

uu
WHITAKER
HOUSE

proclaiming the power of the Gospel through the written word
visit our website at www.whitakerhouse.com

The Practice of God's Presence
Andrew Murray

Is something missing in your Christian life? Do you long to become the person God wants you to be, to feel His presence and experience His power? Andrew Murray's scriptural insights make it easy for you to know God. Learn how to have a dynamic, joy-filled relationship with the Lord. Live every day, every hour, in intimate fellowship with Him. In this collection of six of Murray's best-sellers, you will discover that not only can you have an effective prayer life, but you can also experience the fullness of the Holy Spirit, a blameless heart, and victory over sin.

ISBN: 0-88368-590-6 • Trade • 576 pages

W
WHITAKER
HOUSE

proclaiming the power of the Gospel through the written word
visit our website at www.whitakerhouse.com